When I Were a Lass...

When I Were a Lass...

Joan Bradshawe

PORTICO

First published in the United Kingdom in 2012 by
Portico Books
10 Southcombe Street
London
W14 0RA

An imprint of Anova Books Company Ltd

ISBN 13: 978-1-907554-58-2

A CIP catalogue record for this book is available from
the British Library.

10 9 8 7 6 5 4 3 2 1

Reproduction by Rival Colour Ltd.
Printed and bound by 1010 Printing International Limited, China

This book can be ordered direct from the publisher.
Contact the marketing department, but try your bookshop first.

www.anovabooks.com

Contents

We Were Always Scrubbing

Is it just me – but when I were a lass, I can remember we were always washing. Come rain or shine we'd be outside with bath of hot water and mangle. When we got a twin tub it was like Apollo 11 had landed in our kitchen.

It was one of first things they taught you in school. Forget Pythagoras' theorem lass, this is how you get stuff washed. They taught you with little dolls...

They taught you with unfeasibly big dolls.

11

And if you were a virtuoso with scrubbing brush and carbolic, you got to tackle the problem stains on Big Ted for benefit of rest of class. In them days every school had its Kim and Aggie.

13

Mind you, the old days were very dirty.
We were always getting dirty as a chimney sweep
doing little chores about the house.

And when you got your first ever Easter egg there was this enormous temptation to stuff it all in at once.

17

We knew what was going to happen afterwards.

19

School Were An Education

Of course, you learned a lot more than washing
in school. You learned many many things.
You learned that Jesus was our saviour.

You learned that hacksaws were a lot sharper than they looked.

If you couldn't play netball or hockey, you learned that the PE teacher was a bit of a sadist.

And that some little girls just loved to show off.
I wonder what happened to that Carol Vorderman...?

27

You learned that no matter how well you did
your classwork, it would always be copied
by Fat Angela.

29

And that losing your two front teeth wasn't
the end of the world.

We Loved Our Pets

When I were a lass, pets were top. You didn't have electronic games, computers and endless gizmos to keep you amused. You had a pet. And you could give it a great big cuddle.

Even if it were fish.

Or tortoise.

You shared things with your pet. You could pretend
you were down Milk Bar – like your big sister,
listening to Tommy Steele on jukebox – by sharing
a lovely glass of milk with 'Shane' the kitten.

40

You could get your pet to take you for a spin in your pedal car – just so long as he didn't spot next door's cat. Then it got a bit bumpy...

Doctors and nurses were a favourite game.
Guinea Pig didn't mind being the guinea pig.
He knew the only medicine you could administer
was a carrot.

Rabbit wasn't a big fan of having his temperature taken via the alternative method, but he soon learned to live with it.

People say children can be very cruel to animals, but the dog really didn't mind having his own special 'snake scarf'.

The St. Bernards loved applying layers of thick saliva on your brother's favourite cricket ball.

And Gladys Holroyd's spaniel had no idea she was calculating the velocity needed to get it over next door's fence.

But frog stamping was taking things a bit too far.

Our Love Of Donkeys

The girls in posh Enid Blyton books always used to dream about having a pony and winning first prize at a gymkhana. All we wanted was a donkey.

From the moment we rode one across
the sands on Blackpool beach our hearts
were filled with donkey love.

Even if they did have half an eye on your choc-ice.

You felt like you could tell them your inner most
secrets and they would understand.

Horses were giddy, fickle creatures, liable to toss their heads and gallop off in a moment. Donkeys stood there all nice and quiet - waiting to be loved.

They came in all sizes – big donkeys,
medium donkeys, little donkeys.
With or without a precious load.

Oh yes, the posh girls could sniff, but you'd be proud as punch when you came home with the gold rosette from Donkey of the Year show.

67

The Magic Of Dance

Within every little girl there is a ballet dancer waiting to get out. It's no different today from when I were a lass.

When we started out, we didn't know our
arabesque from our elbow. One girl would be
very good and we'd all try and copy her.
(Even the one that looked like David Cameron.)

71

And then, in the years to come,
we'd all bitterly resent her.

73

The government put a lot of money into dancing back then. On Friday afternoons there were always a dance demonstration going on in lane. It could be ballet, jazz, tap or modern ballroom. We caught the bug.

I always wonder what happened to this skinny
lad called Len we met at the Empire Ballroom...

Dressing Up

One of our big treats was dressing up all Sunday smart. One day, we knew we were going to be ladies.

Like the lady at the big house – who was so posh
she had a tricycle.

We already had tricycles. And frocks, and ribbons.
All we were missing was the big house.

83

You could dress up in all sorts of costumes at local photographer's studio. You could be a Victorian flower girl, a princess, a mermaid, or a rowdy cowgirl with your faithful horse 'Wiggo'.

If you took part in local carnival,
they'd supply the costume for you.

Fame and glamour eh –
all wrapped up in one heady
afternoon of unconfined joy

It was so much better than 'Oak Apple Day' when they made you carry a bundle of twigs and dress like Miss Marple. Even at four years old you realized you looked rubbish.

High Days And Holidays

When I were a lass nobody went on holiday by plane.
You went by train or charabanc, or by bike.
Dad said it saved money. Mum said it wasn't great to
have her cheek glued to his backside for seventy miles.

You could go to seaside on a day trip with school. It were grand to sit on the shingle and listen to the sound of the sea with your best friend Kerry.

In them days, dads had no concept of beachwear.

Or which animals scared the living
daylights out of you.

Or how terrifying it was to be lost in the zoo.
When your parents disappeared, you thought
you'd lost them forever.

They had a wishing seat at our zoo.
You could wish for anything you wanted, provided it involved a white horse and a castle. And didn't involve the sudden disappearance of your school staff room and annoying girls called Janet.

CHILDREN'S WISHING SEAT ZOO

In them days they were free and easy with access to animals. You could wander in and feed anything you liked, provided it were shorter than you.

The fleas you picked up from zoo animals
were real quality items. Much better than your
common or garden dog and cat fleas.
These were bites you could really show off at school.

We Enjoyed Our Hobbies

But you didn't have to go a long way to have fun.
There was a great deal of satisfaction to be had in
growing vegetables that weighed more than your sister.
And were better looking.

We had all the fun of the Flashing Blades ice rink
– if you could be persuaded to let go of the side.

Not to mention the joy of frantic hula hoop
sessions at the local church hall.

Or cross-country hula hoop jumping.
How did that never catch on...?

113

We had swimming at the local pool. Unheated.
It were great fun, providing you could avoid the
showy-off diving girls and the occasional iceberg.

115

You could spend frosty days inside,
knitting the world's first
combined wig/scarf/jumper.

116

If you fancied going into the forces one day,
you could join the sea cadets.
It taught you many valuable skills.

Like how to man the lifeboats and escape
a sinking building.

We Longed To Be Like Our Older Sisters

We worshipped our older sisters. They did everything first. We wanted to be just like them and have trendy hairdos at the salon, while reading a much-thumbed copy of *Woman's Own*.

123

We wanted to have a crush on
John, Paul, George and Ringo.

And scream our heads off at the Odeon.

They were daft, too.
Me sister Joyce never got the
hang of being a milkmaid.

129

And cousin Mable lost her scholarship to a posh school because of some accident nobody in the family would talk about.

They'd play daft games, like bicycle netball.

And when they went busking, the daft beggars walked around instead of standing still and putting cap out. Not that they had a cap.

It's Christmas!

Christmas were the best time of year. We'd go into Municipal Gardens and chop down a lovely tree.

We had no interest in the three wise men as they
weren't taking requests for new dolls' houses
or a premium selection box.

I never quite worked out what Santa was
doing working in a dolls' head factory,
but I was scared to ask too many questions
in case I got put on his blacklist.

But I could definitely tell the difference between Santa and the dog. I knew full well that Santa's breath shouldn't smell of Pedigree Chum.

Picture Credit Where Picture Credit's Due

Pictures courtesy of Getty Images: Pages 11, 14, 21, 25, 27, 29, 33, 37, 49, 51, 55, 57, 61, 67, 68, 73, 79, 81, 85, 91, 92, 97, 101, 103, 105, 106, 113, 114, 119, 123, 129, 134, 137, 139, 141, 143.
Pictures courtesy of Mirrorpix: Pages 2, 7, 9, 19, 23, 31, 35, 45, 58, 63, 65, 71, 75, 76, 83, 86, 87, 89, 95, 99, 109, 111, 117, 121, 125, 126, 133.
Pictures courtesy of Corbis: Pages 13, 17, 39, 40, 43, 47, 52, 131
Cover image: Mirrorpix

Other books in the series:

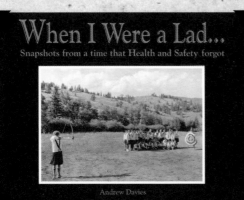